TANGIBLE

He Is

Copyright © 2024 Mary Mora-Babineaux

All rights reserved. ISBN: 9798333300805

Table of Contents

Thou hast turned for me my mourning into dancing:
thou hast put off my sackcloth, and girded me with
gladness; Psalms 30:11 KJV

Introduction

Welcome to **"Tangible He Is: Experiencing the Presence of God in Everyday Life."** This book is a heartfelt exploration of the many ways we can perceive and experience the presence of God in our daily lives. In a world filled with noise and distractions, it can be challenging to recognize the subtle and profound ways in which the divine touches our existence.

The journey to experiencing God is not reserved for the spiritual elite or the deeply religious. It is accessible to everyone, regardless of where you are on your spiritual path. **"Tangible He Is"** is an invitation to open your heart and mind, to look beyond the ordinary and see the extraordinary presence of God in your life.

Within these pages, you will discover:

- **My Personal Testimony**: Stories when I have encountered God's presence in transformative ways.
- **Spiritual Practices:** Practical guidance on prayer, meditation, and mindfulness to help you cultivate a deeper awareness of God.
- **Reflective Insights:** Thought-provoking reflections that encourage you to see the divine in everyday moments.
- **Encouraging** Wisdom: Inspirational quotes and teachings that uplift and strengthen your faith.

2

This book is not just about reading; it is about experiencing. As you delve into each chapter, you will find yourself invited to reflect on your own life, to recognize the sacred in the mundane, and to embrace the divine presence that is always with you. Through prayer, meditation, and attentive living, you will learn to see and feel God's presence in new and profound ways.

"Tangible He Is" is a testament to the belief that God is actively involved in our lives. His presence can be felt in moments of joy and sorrow, in the beauty of nature, in the kindness of others, and in the quiet whispers of our hearts. By opening ourselves to these experiences, we can deepen our faith and find a greater sense of peace and purpose.

"In every heartbeat, in every moment, He is there." Join me on this journey of discovery and realization. Let us explore together the tangible presence of God and celebrate the ways He makes Himself known in our lives. May this book be a source of inspiration, reflection, and profound connection with the divine.

Welcome to **"Tangible He Is: Experiencing the Presence of God in Everyday Life**." May it guide you to a deeper understanding and experience of God's loving presence.

CHAPTER 1

BLOODLINE

I came from a long line of spiritual women…and then there was me. Mary Irene Mora. My middle name "Irene" means peace in (Hebrew) "Eirene". From a very young age, I realized that there was something very special about the women in our family. It was easy to see the unusual level of love. God was tangible in their lives and the impact of their legacy has indelibly imprinted my life.

One of my earliest memories of my great grandmother is from the age of eight, viewing my great grandmother's 94 year old Indian/Hispanic body in the box in her living room. My family was surrounded by people. I know now that these people were only some of the many who loved my great grandmother.

I called her Ama Grande'. She was always so special to me because she made me feel special. I now realize that she had touched many others in the same way. Ama Grande' was a spiritual intercessor and God used her to heal people in her small community of Kingsville, Texas. In my young mind it was overwhelming to see how many people loved her. I heard them describe how Ama Grande' was available as a prayer warrior, midwife or even friend 24 hours a day. She had an amazing heart for people.

Then there was "Ama Chita", my grandmother who was also named "Francisca". Like her mother, she grew up with supernatural strength that came from trusting God. She was emotionally strong but physically weak. She had health issues that impacted her throughout the majority of her life. The doctors never fully understood what was wrong.

Health issues weren't Ama Chita's only problem. Her husband was an alcoholic. One night he got the brilliant idea to walk 45 miles from Kingsville, Texas to Corpus Christi. Tragically, on his way home, from a bar he was struck by a vehicle and lost his life.

Ama chita would say, "God is our strength and comfort." She would frequently add, "Tenemos que dárselo todo a Dios" – which means "we have to give it all to God." Ama chita gave birth to nine children but two passed away when they were babies and her son died on the operating table in his 30's. She knew what it was like to have life not work out well and still chose to fully rely on God.

Even though Ama chita struggled with her health she lived to a ripe old age of 80.

My mother, was the oldest of Ama chita's children. She was born in Kingsville, Texas. At the age of six years old, she had the task of learning how to cook, clean, sew and, so much. She would stand on a stool to help her father cook. She was given tremendous responsibility at a very young age and accepted it gladly.

She came to know the Lord at a very young age, grew steadily in her relationship with him and continued to walk closely with him throughout her life.

My mother was a hard worker and that ethic drove her to develop many varying skills that would later contribute to her survival. She would pick cotton or grain all day. After a long day in the fields she would come home and prepare an amazing meal and then do laundry. Mom never complained.

Like Ama chita, my mother did not have an easy life. In addition to the hard work, she lost her first child, a daughter named Mary Irene, at the age of eight months. My parents had a total of eight children. I was the 7th child and I was also named, Mary Irene.

 Manuel Nava-Mora was my father's name. He was born in Vanderbilt, Texas.

My father was a proud and hardworking man who was expected to help in the cotton fields from a young age. In his twenties he decided to purchase a dump truck to haul sandy loam. My mother would ride with him so she could read the map. You see, dad had a second-grade education and my mother only completed the fifth grade.

It was in March of my eleventh-grade year that my father was diagnosed with cancer. When I found out daddy had cancer I had mixed emotions.

I loved my dad but resented him horribly. When I was 12 years old, we discovered that daddy was having an affair. I was tremendously close to my mother and, therefore, devastated by the pain she experienced. It was during this time that I became aware of what a prayer warrior she was. She wanted to stay faithful to God and chose to be faithful to my father.

Some part of me wanted my father to hurt. Sadly, I experienced a peace in knowing he would never hurt my mother again. Regardless of his faults, I was sad because that was still my daddy.

By the time I was 16, I was driving my daddy to the hospital in my Chevrolet Nova. In my new found freedom as a driver and his weakness through the disease, we bonded like never before. Taking dad to his radiation treatments made me feel close to him.

Daddy made it very clear that his goal was to see me graduate before he died. My parents were careful to provide me with an education that they were not blessed with. The challenge was that his cancer was aggressive, and I still had 3 months for the current year of school and one full year of school remaining.

His dream became my passion. I spoke to a counselor and was allowed to take summer classes. I graduated a year early.

CHAPTER 2

TURNING POINT

My father attended graduation in his wheelchair. He said, "Now you can become a nurse so you can take care of me."

I might have a high school diploma but in my parent's eyes, I was still not old enough to date. After graduation my family and a boy that I liked went to dinner. Dinner that night was a beautiful celebration.

Daddy died four months later, on September 23, 1976.

On his dying bed he asked my mother to forgive him. She had already forgiven him, but he gave her such a beautiful gift when he acknowledged regret for the pain he had caused..father loved his family very much. He passed away when I was 17 years old of colon cancer. It s very difficult for me to process his sudden illness and death. But God!

Only two short years later my family was crushed by the next crisis. My oldest brother, Manuel, committed suicide at the age of 38. He was a private man with a high ranking in the Air Force. We knew he had marital issues but had no idea he was severely depressed. It was approximately 10 years after his death that my brothers told me Manuel did not believe in God.

As a teenager I had miscellaneous jobs. My first was working at a bakery at the age of 15. After high school I attended Del Mar College and became a nurse's assistant. I spent a few years as a nurse's aide then eventually a nurse. I had registered in Kingsville to start the RN program but couldn't bear to leave my mother.

When I finally chose a career, I became a phlebotomist and was still operating as a nurse. I knew having experience as a nurse and in Phlebotomy would be a stronger career path financially. I had chosen to follow dad's wishes in the medical field. I think daddy would have been proud.

Church attendance was not negotiable for my family. Coming from this amazing lineage of spiritual women and very protective parents, you would think I would grow up strong in faith.

As the second youngest of eight children and the only living girl, I had plenty of people to keep me out of trouble.

As a teenager I sat in church but did not have God in my heart. There was no doubt in my mind that God existed but He seemed elusive.

When I struggled or became insecure, instead of turning to the godly women I knew, I began seeking affection from men. I had children young and got married.

My first husband spent four years in the military in Kingsville, Texas. Soon after we married, his military career was over, and he opted to return to his home state of Florida. He also decided he no longer wanted to be married. He wanted a divorce, but I was not going to have it. I followed him to Florida, whether he liked it or not.

CHAPTER 3

BUT GOD

Getting a job in Florida was clearly God's favor. When I arrived for my interview, I was informed that the job had already been filled. The following day I received a call from the lady I had met. She said, "I just feel like I'm supposed to hire you." I didn't understand it at the time but God had placed me under the wings of a spiritual mentor, Sandy Goldberg. Having Sandy in my life was a blessing. Things at home weren't so good. I was hooked on my husband but he was hooked on drugs. I knew it was time to plan an escape when the physical abuse began.

One day I finally gave my husband an ultimatum, "It's either me or the drugs." He made his choice and it wasn't his family. Sandy was a sounding board through this period. She not only became a good friend but she allowed the girls and I to move in once she discovered my situation. While we were living with Sandy I worked two jobs. I was at the hospital working during the day and retail at night. My daughters were 3 and 5 and I was only 26 years old.

Sandy saw to it that we were in church. One day during a service Sandy said, "Mary, do you want to go to the altar and give yourself to God?" I said "yes." I had no earthly idea what was going to come next but I knew I was a mess, and something had to change. I wish I could say that there was an instant radical transformation. That was not my reality. I wanted to be less of a mess but I didn't know where to begin. I had always believed in God but I wanted more than faith that God existed.

I have heard plenty of sermons in my lifetime. I knew God was not just sitting in Heaven waiting for us to get there. I knew a few people that clearly experienced God on a level that I could only imagine. They spoke about having a personal relationship with God. They weren't perfect but they exuded a peace that I could not imagine. Their love of Christ was obvious even when their circumstances weren't good. God was not elusive to them.

It turned out I was only in Florida for about a year. My brother, Clem, came to bring the girls and I back to Corpus once it became clear there was no chance of reconciliation. My brother helped me get an apartment and a new season began.

I wish I could say life was "happily ever after" from that moment forward. I was an utter mess at times. I felt like a failure because of my broken marriage. I felt fear because of financial stress. The thing that propelled me through most days was knowing that I had to create a new life for my children.

I was so numb from all of the mess that I had trouble focusing on God. I didn't feel God was close. Much of my attention was focused on my failure and fear. I couldn't grasp His love. I didn't know what to do to get closer to God. I knew in my head that God was real, but he still felt elusive. I wasn't sure God even loved me because I knew I had made so many poor decisions. I certainly didn't feel worthy of His love. The roller coaster of my life was so drastic because I was searching for God one moment then running from Him the next because of my shame.

I was between husbands and feeling alone. During this time, I was still sitting in a church every Sunday. I was supposed to experience peace as a Christian but I wasn't. There was a bible sitting on my nightstand, but I was following my will, not God's. I felt I had shamed my mother and brothers. It was especially hard disappointing my brother Israel because he was very much a father figure in my life.

I was lying in bed one night and felt compelled to read the bible. I opened it randomly to Psalm 23 and began reading.

The Lord is my shepherd, I shall not want.

He maketh me to lie down in green pastures:

He leadeth me beside the still waters.

He restoreth my soul: He leadeth me in the paths of righteousness for his name's sake.

Yea, though I walk through the valley of the shadow of death, I will fear no evil:

For thou art with me; thy rod and thy staff they comfort me.

I do not know how to describe what happened as I read those words. I felt overwhelmed knowing these were God's words to me. They were holy. He was holy. I felt loved and protected

CHAPTER 4

MY SECURITY MY PROTECTION

The words "valley of the shadow of death" seemed to jump off the page. Over the next few months I realized I had heard from God through his Word for the first time. I somehow knew that God was allowing me to know that I was going to lose my mother soon. Within a year she was gone. No terminal illness, no warning except that warning from God.

The book on the nightstand was no longer for security and protection in my mind. It finally came alive and became a way that a holy God spoke to me. God had allowed me to realize for the first time that he wasn't elusive after all. For the first time in my life, I wanted to do more than just believe in God. I wanted to experience Him personally. I wanted to be fully surrendered. I wanted to walk with Him and allow him to call the shots.

God had used his word to prepare me for the loss of my mother. It was getting weird! God was starting to speak to me.

From that moment forward God would send Christian women to bring me under their wings. I would notice how they drew closer to God. I would cling to their words and ask them questions about their relationship with Christ.

Maria was the first of these women. She was a receptionist at a doctor's office where I worked. It was easy to see the peacefulness of her spirit from the moment we met. I know now she was full of the Holy Ghost.

I saw the love of Christ in Maria. I saw her passion for knowing God.

One week I got the flu. I remember Maria randomly showing up at my house with homemade chicken soup. God allowed me to see agape love through her. It blew me away. I was seeing what it was like to know someone who allowed Christ to live through them.

Many months after we met, she finally confessed that when we first met God had told her to "take me under her wings."

She would share her experiences. I could see and feel something different in her. I didn't know how to become more like Maria but I wanted to.

She started inviting me to conferences. One year we were at a conference in San Antonio, Texas where people were speaking in tongues. That was new to me. It was unusual but not uncomfortable.

After the conference Maria said, "God told me you are a woman of destiny. He's telling me to tell you." She didn't know my story…my brokenness, shame and feelings of abandonment. I knew she had to have heard God wrong. There was no question in my mind that God could not use me. There were plenty of people that were more godly.

The enemy was feeding my insecurities. I was flashing back to all the mistakes I had made. Clearly if Maria really knew me, she would have disqualified me.

Maria would just say it over and over with a smile, "You are a woman of destiny." There was always so much love in her expression. She saw my future even when I couldn't see it or accept it.

Not long afterward I attended a three-day women's retreat. My girlfriend, Laura, had asked me to go to the retreat. I blindly said, "yes." I had absolutely no clue what I was saying yes to. I had learned to trust God and the Christians he put in my life.

This weekend was a pivotal moment for me. Away from the distractions of my daily life I experienced God's presence on a new level. I made a new friend, Michelle. She was loving and compassionate. Experiencing God's love through Michelle allowed me to believe that I could be closer to God.

I didn't want to ever leave this place. God was wooing me. I begged God to let me stay there. I wanted to be closer to Him and serve people. I was never the same after that.

I was allowed to be part of the planning team on the next three-day retreat. That is where I met Ana. I connected to her because I saw that crazy peaceful spirit in her. We had a lot in common including each having a brother that was an alcoholic. We would pray for each and for our brothers. Drugs and alcohol were to become a tremendous problem in my family.

It wasn't long after meeting Ana that I first was provided clear direction from God. This should have been an exciting experience but he was asking me to do something that I did not want to do. I was at home praying one night when I heard God say in my spirit, "go to your brother's house and pray." I was asking God for an assignment, but I didn't like this one.

I somewhat politely began to argue with God. "Lord, surely you don't want me to go to his house. He and his wife are both on drugs. We aren't even on speaking terms. I will pray for him here." I heard God say, "You're asking me where I want you to start. I am telling you where I want you to go." I called my friend, Ana. She was used to hearing from God. Ana encouraged me to be obedient and asked if I wanted her to go with me. Of course, I said yes. I called my sister-in- law and asked her if I could come pray for them. She sounded desperate, lonely and scared. Surprisingly she said, "yes, please come."

That was not the response I expected. I knew immediately that God was talking to me and at the same time, working on their hearts. I still expected that my brother was going to be his usual, mean self. As Ana and I arrived at their home I should have been excited about my first assignment from God. I was, however, focused on my fears. I had wrestled with God about this assignment, but He had won.

As we entered the house, I could tell they were under the influence of drugs. You could feel the darkness in their home. This was when I learned that the enemy was real and present.

This was my first exposure to evil on that level. I didn't know what to do. I sat on the floor while Ana spoke to them about God's love. Ana didn't know them but I know now she was with me to help me to know what to do.

She said, "Your sister loves you and I'm here because I love her." It was like Jesus was there. My brother was in awe. It became obvious that he and my sister-in-law were at their wits end. They listened intently as she expressed love and concern.

I wondered if he was tired of being tormented by the enemy. I cried out of gratitude as I realized they were open to God. Only God could have orchestrated this.

CHAPTER 5

SEEKING GOD IN THE MIDST OF TRAGEDY

The next day I went back with my friend, Maria. They opened up even more as she talked to them about giving their lives to Christ. We walked around the house, took authority and claimed this house for the Lord and rebuked the enemy. At their lowest of lows, they were desperate to know God. They prayed and chose to follow Christ. They had broken the chains of evil dominating their lives. God modeled His peace through Ana and Maria. It occurred to me that I didn't have to know exactly how to handle every situation. I was required to listen to God and obey Him. He would either give me the words or connect me to someone who had them.

Maria and Ana were not the last of the women that God chose to bring into my life. As I chose to draw closer to Him, he began surrounding me with women in their 20's and 30's that were struggling. God allowed me to see the best in them...just as Maria and Ana had seen the best in me.

I have discovered that there is no process for spiritual maturity. There is no formula that we can read in a book and follow. God is a person that wants us to know Him intimately. He will take each of us through different steps as He draws us close to Him. If we are to reach spiritual maturity we need to crave the Creator.

I began attending bible studies and searching for Him. I felt him pursuing me. God became my priority. This is when God really starts unraveling things. This is when I began to be able to experience peace in my life on a deeper level.

Peace came crashing down on July 4, 2008. It was my deceased mother's birthday. My brothers had gone to mom's grave and serenaded her at midnight. Everyone had gone home.

In San Antonio, Texas two of my nephews got into an argument at 4:00 a.m. and my 36-year-old nephew shot and killed his 22-year-old brother. I received a phone call in Corpus early in the morning. The family was not able to reach my brother. I was asked to go to his home and explain that one of his children was dead and the other in jail.

I was in shock. I knew I had to hurry to my brother's side. I couldn't imagine breaking the news. I was in the car by myself driving. I kept begging God to give me the right words. I called my friend Maria and her husband answered. Maria wasn't home but they were both pastors and I knew they would both be praying.

The drive was a blur. I was driving and praying for guidance. I was begging that God would provide my brother with strength. I have no idea what words came out of my mouth. When my brother found out that he had lost his son he fell to his knees and began screaming for our mother. He screamed that it was his fault because he had sent his younger son to live with the older one.

I drove my brother to San Antonio as quickly as I could. We prayed the entire way. When we entered the house where my nephew had been shot, the essence of evil was overwhelming. We did not stay long. The next stop was the hospital. The trauma doctor in the Emergency Room came to us and described that Francisco was dead when he arrived at the hospital. He had experienced multiple bullet wounds and one hit him in the heart.

All of the family bawled hysterically as we viewed the body in the morgue. His sister, Vanessa, and his mother had flown in from California. Vanessa stood over the body with her bible open and read Psalm 23. The same scripture God had given me a year before my mother died. Vanessa had no idea that scripture had such a tremendous impact on my life when I lost my mom. She explained to us that Francisco had recently accepted Christ. She had sent him a bible from California. There was overwhelming peace as we finally knew he was with Jesus.

My brother Israel had to bury one son and worry about the possibility of the other son spending the rest of his life in prison. By God's grace, the older son ended up not serving any time. I prayed for my brother constantly and tried to console him. I couldn't imagine how he would ever recover from this.

CHAPTER 6

LEANING ON GOD'S UNCHANGING HAND

Shortly thereafter, my mother-in-law was struggling with health issues. I felt led by God to invite her to live with my husband Robert and I. She moved into our Corpus home. I quit my job to help take care of my husband's mom. She struggled with kidney and heart issues. God showed me that I needed to show her Jesus' love.

Momma Margie was a homemaker. She would help work at the gas station her husband owned and sell baked goods. Her husband died because of heart issues when he was only 49 years old.

Margie was a widow with five children at home. She eventually remarried and lost that husband to leukemia. Not long afterward she lost one son when he went into the hospital for minor day surgery and died with heart issues. Tragically she had to bury a son who died of AIDS.

Momma Margie struggled but masked her pain. She was a beautiful soul. Everyone felt loved when they were with her. She was an amazing hostess and a blessing to be around.

Robert's mother, however, did not always have church as a priority in her life. Through all the pain she had built up walls and was not experiencing the love of Christ. The Holy Spirit told me clearly that I was to show her the love of God.

When Margie moved to our home, our new normal was Momma Margie and I at home with Robert going to work. We did this for three years in Corpus then felt led by God to move to Dallas to be closer to the children and grandchildren living there. It was in Dallas in 2014 that Momma Margie died.

CHAPTER 7

I CHOOSE TO TRUST GOD

With the house quiet and no major obligations nor work, I had to learn to be still with God. Quiet time and time in the Word allowed me to be in a wonderful place with God. In September 2014 I was on the way home from a mission trip to Guatemala when my friend, Laura and I began sharing that we had each heard clearly from God that we were to raise money to build a home in Guatemala. God was clear that we were to donate to Potter's House in Guatemala City as they had a strong building program. For only $5,000 they could put a family in a home. We planned to raise funds and return to help with the construction.

Robert and I had asked friends to donate unwanted items and had many garage sales to raise funds for the home we were to build in Guatemala. As I continued in prayer, I was thanking God for the overwhelming support as donations continued to flow in. I knew that the many items that had been donated for our garage sales were definitely from God. My husband, Robert and I were preparing for a mission trip to Guatemala.

I went back to work part-time and got back into a routine. Our routine life soon changed radically. In June 2015 I was in between patients at work. I was reading and praying. Out of nowhere I heard, "You are about to be UNDONE!"

Not the words that you want to hear, particularly when you know they are from God. After my assignment with my brother I was used to wonderful experiences with God. Not every word from God was 100% what

I would have wished but I trusted Him to always work out every situation for good.

My mind raced. What did "undone" mean? I expected my life was getting ready to be upset drastically. I knew I had not been feeling great for the last year but I'd been focusing on others and life had been chaotic with my mother-in-law's declining health and passing. I hadn't really paid attention to my health. I had no choice but to stay close to God and see what happened next. I knew that God is good and had always been faithful. I trusted him.

One morning I was pacing outside in the garage. I was overwhelmed with all the donations. I was excited about the trip and praising God when He said, "You're not going to Guatemala." This crushed me. I asked God, "Why?" There was no answer. I could only wait and trust.

We had been raising money for months for the home to be built. I wanted to see my sponsored child, Joshua, when we visited Guatemala. It made no sense. I had clearly heard from God that this house was to be built and had worked tirelessly to raise money. I couldn't imagine why I wasn't going to be able to go.

When I arrived home that evening I explained the experience to Robert. By this time, he was used to me hearing from God. We had no idea what was to come but we could only spend time together in prayer and trust God.

We continued to obediently raise money for the home to be built in Guatemala and waited to see what the Lord had in store. Several months later I began having headaches. By June 2015 they started becoming more frequent. I originally thought it was sinus headaches but began to wonder. My appetite was decreasing but I didn't think much of it.

One day I had gone to spend time with a girl that God had led me to minister to. We had a great time then I got in my car to drive home. On the drive I had a horrific headache. By the time I got home I was feeling really bad. It was after lunch, and I decided to take a nap. Robert was not working so he laid down beside me. I felt God say, "It is time now."

I explained to Robert, "It's time to go to the emergency room. Something is seriously wrong." He was taken aback because I was not one to complain about health. As a pharmacist he went into fix it mode. He said, "Do you need an antibiotic? Do you want me to get you an ice pack?"

I said yes to the ice pack even though I expected it wasn't going to help at all. Robert, however, was right, the ice pack provided relief. Even with the relief I felt a tugging in my spirit that it was time to go to the hospital. I told Robert, "We need to go to the emergency room now."

We headed to the hospital and went through triage. Unfortunately, we spent a ton of time in the waiting room of the emergency room. I was frustrated and wanted to leave but then heard God say, "Start praying for the sick." I had a horrible headache, but I was obedient and was praying for the sick. My frustration levels eventually got the best of me. I went to the lady at the desk and told her I was going to leave. She informed me that I could not leave, and I had been identified as a "high risk." I already knew something was wrong, but this was clarification that it was probably serious.

When I finally got back to the room, I was excited to see the nurse that came in to greet me. She had an angelic appearance and had on camouflage scrubs. As a prayer warrior and a person who was familiar with spiritual battles...I felt like God had sent her to me personally.

I was taken back for a CT scan. Then we waited for the results. When the doctor came back he began to tell me how healthy I was. I stopped him and said, "OK, what's wrong with me?" Then there were those dreaded words, "You've got a brain tumor."

Instead of the anticipated meltdown, I said, "OK, what do we need to do next? Let's take care of it."

The next two days were more tests including an MRI. They prescribed me with steroids because they said my brain was already swelling.

The neurosurgeon later explained to my husband that the tumor was putting pressure on my brain and could cause me to have seizures. He warned Robert not to leave me alone.

Shortly thereafter I began feeling numbness in my arm.

By tis time I was definitely feeling undone.

Back at home I spent time with God. I chose to be at peace. I remembered that this earth is not my home. I chose to trust God. As I approached God in my quiet time he told me, "There is something wrong but I will use it."

One day Robert, my brother Israel and I were in our living room. God told me to go outside. I was getting used to hearing from the Holy Spirit now.

I explained to them that I was going outside to the front to take a walk. They both hesitated because they were afraid of me having seizures. After a little coaxing I convinced them, I would be fine.

He sent his word, and healed them, and delivered them from their destructions.

Psalm 107:20 KJV

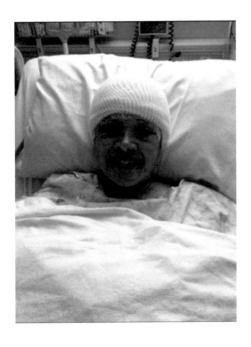

And he said unto her, Daughter, thy faith hath made thee whole; go in peace, and be whole of thy plague.

Mark 5:34 KJV

CHAPTER 8

HE TOUCHED ME

I took a stroll in the front yard. It was a peaceful place to be with God. While strolling I heard the Spirit say, "I'm going to be so tangible to you." I ran inside and told Robert and Israel. I asked them what they thought it meant. They came up with some theories on what God meant by being "tangible." I got down on my knees and explained to them "I believe He's literally going to put his arms around me and touch me."

What followed was an amazing week as God was preparing me for my surgery. My daughters were now grown and they showed me love and support. My family and friends were there for me.

My friend Tina Myers was a constant companion and tremendous inspiration. She came to my home one day and I was sitting at the kitchen table. She explained to me that she had asked the Holy Spirit what she was supposed to do that day. She handed me some heart earrings. She told me that God informed her, "You are going to have the heart of Jesus." It brought tears to both our eyes.

I told her, "That's awesome. That's all I want is a heart like Jesus."

Fast forward a couple of days and I got a phone call from another friend named Tina Zarcone. She said, "I know you're going to have a lot of family and friends coming in for your surgery. I want to spend time alone with you before they all get here." I expected that my time with Tina would be time reminiscing about our friendship and the God moments we had shared. What I didn't know is that Tina had also asked the Holy Spirit what she was supposed to do when she got to my house. The Holy Spirit had told her, "I want you to wash her feet."

Washing of feet symbolizes humility and the selfless love of Jesus.

The house already had several family members when Tina arrived. After a while I realized that my daughter Theresa and Tina had disappeared. They were preparing my bedroom with candles, prophetic music and a basin to wash my feet. When she came out most of the visitors had left.

Tina said, "Come on. Let's go into your bedroom." When I walked into the bedroom, everything in my life changed forever.

The minute I walked into the room the Spirit of God hit me so hard that I fell into the chair that was next to my bed. As I fell, immediately my hands went into the air.

Tina explained to my daughter, Theresa, that she needed to wash my feet.

Theresa protested by saying, "But God told you to do it Tina." She said, "You are her daughter. You need to wash her feet."

I later learned from Tina that Theresa was washing my

feet and praying over me in tongues.

After Theresa was finished then Tina began washing my feet and praying over me.

I was overcome with the presence of God. I was overwhelmed with His love. The Spirit had taken me.

I felt the hands of Jesus touching me. He touched me all over my face and my eyes. He used my hands to touch my face. I could feel Him touching me.

He then began to touch me all over my body. He wanted me to feel His love. He wanted me to fully comprehend His love. He wanted me to experience the love that I lacked from my daddy.

He then began to work on my heart. I felt Him pulling bitterness, unforgiveness, guilt, shame, insecurity and everything that was not of Him. Those wounds were removed and replaced with His pure love. God allowed me to experience his presence in a very tangible way.

Through the experience Tina was asking God for direction. He told her to get my husband and bring him into the room. I remember Robert coming in and beginning to wash my feet. By then I was drunk in the Spirit and could not stop laughing. As Robert was washing my feet, Tina said he kept asking her, "Am I tickling her?"

Tina explained, "No, that is just the Spirit."

The brain tumor had brought me closer to my husband than I had been in years. Robert laid his head on my stomach. The Spirit was manifest in a huge way.

There were hours of the Spirit touching me. Hours of experiencing His love. I didn't ever want it to stop.

Family members came into the bedroom and let me know that more company had arrived. I didn't want to leave the room. I didn't want to leave His presence. It was me and God.

Eventually Tina kissed me and said goodbye.

I spent time with friends, but I couldn't think about anything except being back in my bedroom with God. I experienced God with me and in me like never before.

My family decided I needed to eat and insisted that we go out to eat. I really wasn't interested but had no ability to dispute the decision. I was still in a daze and was still experiencing God like never before.

In the car my daughter Theresa said, "Didn't my mom like Lionel Richie?" My friend, Belay, said, "Oh yes. How about the song Hello...is it me you're looking for?"

That song came on the radio, and I felt like God was speaking to me. I felt God telling me, "My eye has been on you since you were a little girl." God gave me a vision that He had been wooing me since I was a little girl. He showed me that He knew all my pain. He understood my brokenness.

I could hear the words, "Is it me you're looking for?" I remembered all the times I searched for Him but felt alone. At the restaurant I obediently picked at my food. I wanted so badly to get back to my bedroom.

We arrived back home at almost midnight. I spent the next few hours in my room worshiping and dancing until 2:30 a.m. I remember the Spirit telling me, "OK, you can go lay your head down."He wooed me and held me. I slept for about 30 minutes and then I got up. I woke up clapping my hands. I walked around the house and woke everyone up.

I announced to my family and friends in the house, "OK, let's go get this thing out." My husband stared at me in shock and said, "You know what, you are something else." I kept telling him, "It's God." I was never fearful. I was so joyful. I was preparing to leave while singing worship songs. I will worship you in spirit and truth!

At the hospital I insisted that they take me back to the back. I didn't want to be in the waiting room but alone with God. The receptionist took me to get a CT scan and didn't make me go back to the waiting room with my family and friends. My husband came back to be with me and eventually my family and friends came back to the pre-op room to see me, pray over me, and kiss me on my forehead before I went into surgery. Lots of love filled the waiting room, I was so thankful for the outpouring of love from Jesus.

My friend Tina that had given me the hearts bent to kiss me and started crying. She said, "Oh my. I can see Jesus in your eyes." She kissed me on my forehead, and they all left. The surgery was supposed to be over three hours long. It ended up being only one hour and fifteen minutes. The surgeon said the tumor was easily accessible and he was able to get it out quickly. The doctor came out and informed Robert, "Everything went well. We're taking her into recovery and then ICU."

I had not been on great terms with my daughter, August when I found out about the brain tumor. As soon as the surgery was over, she told Robert, "You go home dad. I want to stay with mom. You go get some sleep." In the ICU I told my oldest daughter August to turn on worship music. I could not stop praising God. August spent the next few days with me, most of the time she laid in bed with me. We were closer than ever.

At home I was recovering and ministering to people that would call and visit, some the lord prompted to come and see me. Papa Yaweh would have a word for them. I was his vessel and I said to him "Use me, Lord." During that time, I still felt closer to God more than ever in my life. Recovery was slow and there were times that I fell and even once I hit my head.

My husband and brother were planning to go to Guatemala. It was difficult knowing that I could not go but I was excited for them. While they were in Guatemala they called when they could and took lots of photos of the home that was being built. It was a home that I knew God wanted built.

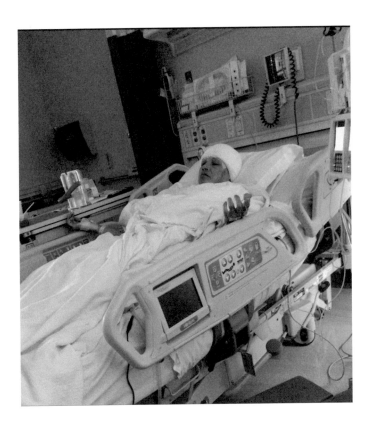

CHAPTER 9

STANDING ON GOD'S WORD

A couple of months later I decided to go from Dallas to Corpus Christi, Texas to visit my daughter and her family. I was feeling worse. At this point in time, it was difficult to read the Word of God and even write my name. My right side was feeling weak. I knew something wasn't right but chose to stay in denial.

I was getting depressed and feeling alone. I wanted to be in Corpus Christi to visit my granddaughter Chloe as she celebrated her 14th birthday.

After a few days with my daughter, Theresa, and her family she said, "Mom, you don't look good." I told her I'd be fine and would visit the doctor when I got home.

The following day Theresa announced that she was not going to work because she was worried about leaving me alone. I insisted that I would be fine, and they needed to go to work.

Once everyone was gone, I tried to get out of bed. I made it to the hall and collapsed. It became clear that something was very wrong. Instead of calling someone, I was determined to take a shower before I dealt with my health.

I finally made it to the shower and fell in the shower. Praise God I did not hit my head with the fall. It took me quite a while to stand up. Eventually I made it out of the shower and decided to try to eat something. After a few bites of soup, I was vomiting.

Theresa walked in the door and told me, "You're going to the hospital." After a lengthy amount of time in the waiting room, we finally got to triage.

The hospital staff didn't seem that concerned and talked about sending me home. Theresa objected until they realized something was wrong. Theresa updated them on my recent surgery and informed them that I could not walk at all. Now they were taking things seriously.

They rushed me to get a CT scan. They were able to see bleeding and I was diagnosed with a subdural hematoma on the left side of my brain. Again, I was rushed to another hospital and taken immediately into surgery. They had to drill into my skull to relieve the pressure.

God said to me clearly, "I will use this. Just trust me."

It was another tangible moment. Many came to visit while I was in ICU. They were able to see the power of God in me. God brought them so I could share His faithfulness and His love. To God be the glory.

He had me on a mountaintop. I was his daughter. I was beginning to understand how much he loved me. I wanted the love of my daddy because I lost my father when I was only 17 years old. God gave me everything I wanted and more.

Now I crave opportunities to worship and dance for God. I crave time with my Lord. I want to continue to be obedient and please him. Praising my Heavenly Father is now a huge part of my heart.

I still struggle with frustrations at times but never question the love and goodness of my Papa. Even in hard times in my life The Lord has been present in accomplishing great things. God told me, "You will tell my people how tangible I am, and this world holds no reward!" The Lord has taught me that when we have surrendered and obey the holy spirit, he is able to heal our deepest wounds. He will never leave us or forsake us. He will finish the work he has begun with us.

God is teaching me to love people as he loves them… Unconditionally. I pray that God continues to allow me to serve in the mission field, community, family, and randomly as he sees fit. I am a work in progress but will continue to seek him with my whole heart, soul, and mind.

Any victory in my life is because Jesus died for me. Our home is not here but in eternity!

I had clearly been "undone." There was no question God had been accurate with those words. He said he would be "tangible." That word "tangible" had fallen into my spirit through my Abba Daddy. Now I knew exactly what He meant...Tangible He Is!

Romans 8:28

And we know that in all things God works for the good of those who love him, who[a] have been called according to his purpose.

God will redeem you from all of your iniquities, missteps and afflictions.

Psalms 130:1-4

Out of the depths I cry to you, Lord; Lord, hear my voice. Let your ears be attentive to my cry for mercy. If you, Lord, kept a record of sins, Lord, who could stand? But with you there is forgiveness, so that we can, with reverence, serve you.

Isaiah 61:3

To [a]console those who mourn in Zion, To give them beauty for ashes,

The oil of joy for mourning,

The garment of praise for the spirit of heaviness; That they may be called trees of righteousness, The planting of the Lord, that He may be glorified."

Hebrews 4:12

For the word of God is living and powerful, and sharper than any two- edged sword, piercing even to the division of soul and spirit, and of joints and marrow, and is a discerner of the thoughts and intents of the heart.

Jeremiah 29:11-12

For I know the thoughts that I think toward you, says the Lord, thoughts of peace and not of evil, to give you a future and a hope. [12] Then you will call upon Me and go and pray to Me, and I will listen to you.

Exodus 4:11-12

So the Lord said to him, *"Who has made man's mouth? Or who makes the mute, the deaf, the seeing, or the blind? Have not I, the Lord? [12] Now therefore, go, and I will be with your mouth and teach you what you shall say."*

The one who call is faithful, and He will do it. God equips those that He calls.

I John 1:9

*If we confess our sins, He is faithful and just to forgive us **our sins and to cleanse us from all unrighteousness.***

2 Corinthians 12:9-10 9

[9]But he said to me, "My grace is sufficient for you, for my power is made perfect in weakness." Therefore I will boast all the more gladly about my weaknesses, so that Christ's power may rest on me. [10]That is why, for Christ's sake, I delight in weaknesses, in insults, in hardships, in persecutions, in difficulties.

Psalm 46:10

Be still, and know that I am God; I will be exalted among the nations, I will be exalted in the earth!

Proverbs 3:5-6

5Trust in the Lord with all your heart, And lean not on your own understanding; 6 In all your ways acknowledge Him, And He shall [a]direct your paths.

John 10:27

My sheep hear My voice, and I know them, and they follow Me.

Jeremiah 29:13-14

13And you will seek Me and find Me, when you search for Me with all your heart. 14I will be found by you, says the Lord, and I will bring you back from your captivity; I will gather you from all the nations and from all the places where I have driven you, says the Lord, and I will bring you to the place from which I cause you to be carried away captive.

The Holy Spirit works in us by peeling away our sinful characteristics and replacing them with Godly characteristics. His work in us makes us more and more like Jesus.

Acts 1:8

But you will receive power when the Holy Spirit comes on you; and you will be my witnesses in Jerusalem, and in all Judea and Samaria, and to the ends of the earth."

Isaiah 42:6

I the Lord have made you the vessel of my purpose, I have taken you by the hand, and kept you safe, and I have given you to be an agreement to the people, and a light to the nations.

Isaiah 43:2

When you pass through the waters, I will be with you; and through the rivers, they shall not overwhelm you; when you walk through fire you shall not be burned, and the flame shall not consume you.

Philippians 1:6

"I am sure of this, that he who began a good work in you will bring it to completion at the day of Jesus Christ. " (Philippians 1:6) (Romans 10:9-10)

"Your legacy is not what you leave for people; it's what you leave in them. Build a life that inspires others to be their best selves."

Peter Strople

..Behold, I will bring it health and cure, and I will cure them, and will reveal unto them the abundance of peace and truth.

Jeremiah 33:6 KJV

My little children, let us not love in word, neither in tongue; but in deed and in truth.

1 John 3:18 KJV

I will get me unto the great men, and will speak unto them; for they have known the way of the LORD, and the judgmen of their God: but these have altogether broken the yoke, and burst the bonds.

Jeremiah 5:5 KJV

He that walketh with wise men shall be wise: ....

Proverbs 13:20 KJV

Iron sharpeneth iron; so a man sharpeneth the countenance of his friend.

Proverbs 27:17

Mary Mora-Babineaux

Mary worked in the medical field for over 22 years. She shared Jesus ' heart as she lovingly cared for patients, while assisting Drs and staff.

She has mentored women of all ages throughout the Christian walk ,as she shares her testimony of God's love through horrific Medical struggles.

Worship and dancing , for Jesus has been a big part of her life. Giving God all the glory, she is bold with her faith as she shares how tangible God is.

Mary's married with a blended family ,of four wonderful children, 12 grandchildren, and two great grandchildren.

But seek ye first the kingdom of God, and his righteousness; and all these things shall be added unto you. Matthew 6:33 (KJV)

Made in the USA
Columbia, SC
21 August 2024

40862429R00035